ANGELINA JOLIE

GOODWILL AMBASSADOR FOR THE UNITED NATIONS

ROSEN
PUBLISHING
New York

LAURA LA BELLA

For Matt

Published in 2009 by The Rosen Publishing Group, Inc.
29 East 21st Street, New York, NY 10010
www.rosenpublishing.com

Library of Congress Cataloging-in-Publication Data

La Bella, Laura.
Angelina Jolie: goodwill ambassador for the United Nations / Laura La Bella.—1st ed.
    p. cm.—(Celebrity activist biographies)
Includes bibliographical references and index.
ISBN-13: 978-1-4042-1762-1 (library binding)
1. Jolie, Angelina, 1975– 2. Motion picture actors and actresses—
United States—Biography. 3. Human rights workers—United
States—Biography. I. Title.
PN2287.J583L3 2009
791.4302'8092—dc22

                                                2007044915

On the cover: Inset: Angelina Jolie at the Venice Film Festival, September 2, 2007. Background: Jolie in her role as Goodwill Ambassador for the United Nations, visiting earthquake survivors at the Gari Habibullah Camp in Pakistan on November 24, 2005.

CONTENTS

INTRODUCTION

I n 2000, Angelina Jolie arrived in Cambodia to begin filming *Lara Croft: Tomb Raider*. A few months later, she left as a woman on a mission to change the world.

In the years since then, the Oscar-winning actress has combined the glamour of Hollywood with the grit of refugee camps. She has traveled to more than twenty different third world countries, where she has spent time in refugee camps identifying the problems refugees face.

As a Goodwill Ambassador for the United Nations High Commissioner for Refugees (UNHCR), an organization that helps nearly fifteen million displaced

In August 2003, Angelina Jolie visited the Bella refugee camp in Ingushetia, a region bordering Chechnya. Above, she takes notes as she looks over the camp and its conditions.

people around the world, Jolie acts in her most inspired role. She has become more than a celebrity with an opinion and a checkbook. In addition to providing financial support herself, Jolie takes a hands-on approach at the refugee camps she visits. She helps feed sick children, transport thousands of refugees to safer camps, build huts of mud, and distribute much-needed food and water.

Each experience leaves her more knowledgeable and more prepared to speak on behalf of the thousands of people who have been forced from their homes and villages. Jolie has met with world leaders to seek support for refugees and refugee-related issues. She has attended countless meetings on Capitol Hill in Washington, D.C., urging the U.S. government to become more involved. In addition, she has donated millions of dollars to organizations around the world—organizations that help support orphans and provide developing countries with medical clinics, medicine, and emergency aid.

Angelina Jolie has also taken her mission to the masses. She has used the media to bring attention to refugees' harrowing stories. She turned her personal journals, chronicling her first three years visiting refugee camps, into a best-selling book; took out a full-page advertisement in *USA Today* to raise national awareness of the conflict in Darfur; and had an opinion-editorial (op-ed) published in the *Washington Post*. She has used her fame not only to bring attention to the needs of refugees but also to conflicted areas around the world that need the help of international peacekeepers.

When Jolie decided to become a mother, she followed the path on which her role as an ambassador has taken her, adopting children from the countries she is striving to help. With her children, each born in a different African or Asian nation, Jolie has become the world's mother figure.

This is Angelina Jolie's crusade to change the world for the better.

CHAPTER ONE

Angelina Jolie and Her Road to Humanitarian Causes

Angelina Jolie is one of the most highly regarded actresses of her generation. By her early thirties, she had already starred in more than forty films, among them box-office blockbusters like *Mr. and Mrs. Smith, The Bone Collector, Gone in 60 Seconds,* and *Lara Croft: Tomb Raider.*

Early in her acting career, Jolie garnered Hollywood's attention by taking on two very daring roles. First, Jolie portrayed supermodel Gia Carangi in HBO's critically acclaimed TV movie *Gia.* The movie chronicled the destruction of Carangi's life as a result of her drug addiction. The role earned Jolie both Golden Globe and Screen Actors Guild awards for her performance. She was also nominated for an Emmy Award.

Jolie followed the success of *Gia* with another powerful performance, this time in the film *Girl, Interrupted*. The role of Lisa Rowe, a flamboyant, irresponsible sociopath, earned Jolie an Academy Award, Hollywood's highest honor. Jolie won the award for Best Supporting Actress. She also took home another set of Golden Globe and Screen Actors Guild trophies.

After such critical successes, Jolie was highly regarded for her acting talent and for her ability to mold seamlessly into a character. However, Jolie had yet to play the lead role in a major Hollywood film. Her next project would change that, putting her at the center of a major motion picture. The experience would also end up widening Jolie's view of the world and permanently changing her life.

A Whole New World

Paramount Pictures was adapting *Tomb Raider*, a popular action-adventure video game, for film. The studio was looking for an actress to take on the lead role of Lara Croft, an antiquities hunter who travels

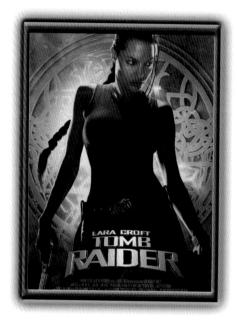

Lara Croft: Tomb Raider hit theaters in 2001. While in Cambodia for the filming of the movie, Jolie was first exposed to the struggles of refugees.

the world in search of treasures and artifacts. Jolie accepted the role, her first in an action-adventure movie.

Lara Croft: Tomb Raider began filming in Angkor, Cambodia. Located in Southeast Asia, the region also contains the nations of Laos, Myanmar, Thailand, and Vietnam. Much to Jolie's surprise, for their safety, the film's cast and crew were restricted from many parts of the landscape in and around the movie's sets. As a result of a civil war, the country has an untold number of still-active land mines. Land mines are devices that are placed either on or in the ground. They explode when triggered by an operator, or by a vehicle, person, or animal that is in the proximity of the mine itself. Land mines are often used as a military tactic to secure borders during disputes between countries, or to restrict enemy movement in times of war. Cambodia's land is littered with thousands of active land mines.

Jolie was shocked by the presence of the mines. "There were areas we shot in, that we could only be in certain places, because they hadn't been de-mined yet," Jolie said in an interview with the Web site NY Rock. "And to know that there are hospitals where kids are still being affected by stepping on landmines every day, was horrifying and so sad. You never hear about that. To discover that kind of stuff was to really understand people in the rest of the world," she continued. "Cambodia was really eye opening for me."

While in the country, Jolie also became aware of the nation's extreme poverty. Cambodia is one of Asia's poorest countries. More than half of the nation's children are malnourished, and one out of every eight children dies before the age of five. As she learned more about Cambodia, Jolie was stunned, not only by the statistics but also by her own lack of knowledge about the Asian nation and the world as a whole.

To educate herself, after the movie was filmed, Jolie went to Washington, D.C., and sat with officials

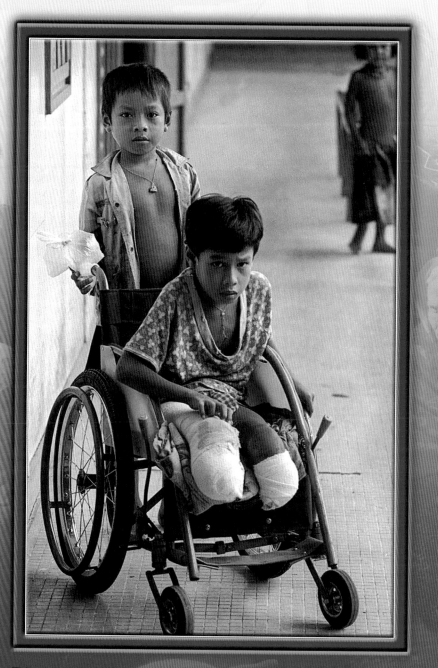

This girl, pictured in a hospital in Cambodia, lost her legs in a land mine accident. Jolie works to raise awareness of land mines in Cambodia and supports organizations that work to locate and safely remove them.

from the Office of the United Nations High Commissioner for Refugees (UNHCR) to learn more about Cambodia and other international trouble spots.

An Organization with a Higher Mission

UNHCR, established on December 14, 1950, by the United Nations General Assembly, is one of the world's principal humanitarian agencies. According to the organization's Web site, UNHCR is "an agency mandated to lead and coordinate international action to protect refugees and resolve refugee problems worldwide." Today, with a staff of more than 6,500 people around the world, UNHCR helps an estimated twenty-one million people in more than 116 countries. For over fifty years, the agency has provided assistance to more than fifty million people and has been awarded two Nobel Peace Prizes.

Jolie approached UNHCR with an interest in not only learning more but also getting involved. "I read about the different chapters [of the United Nations] and UNHCR was the most appealing," Jolie said in an interview posted on the UNHCR Web site. "I believe refugees are the most vulnerable people in the world. They are affected by everything."

Basic Facts About UNHCR

UNHCR was established by the UN General Assembly in 1950. UNHCR provides protection and assistance to refugees. The agency is funded almost entirely by voluntary contributions, mainly from governments, but also from governmental organizations, corporations, and individuals.

Countries and regions that receive the most help from UNHCR include:

Europe: European nations receive thousands of refugee requests annually.

The Balkans: At least 600,000 people have been uprooted in this politically unstable region.

Palestine: The nation has more than four million refugees worldwide. The vast majority of them are under the care of the UN Relief and Works Agency (UNRWA) in Jordan, Syria, Lebanon, the West Bank, and Gaza.

Iraq: The war-torn nation has more than 1.2 million internally displaced people living inside Iraq, with UNHCR providing emergency assistance.

Afghanistan: With approximately 3.2 million Afghans still remaining in Pakistan and Iran, the country remains UNHCR's largest population concern worldwide.

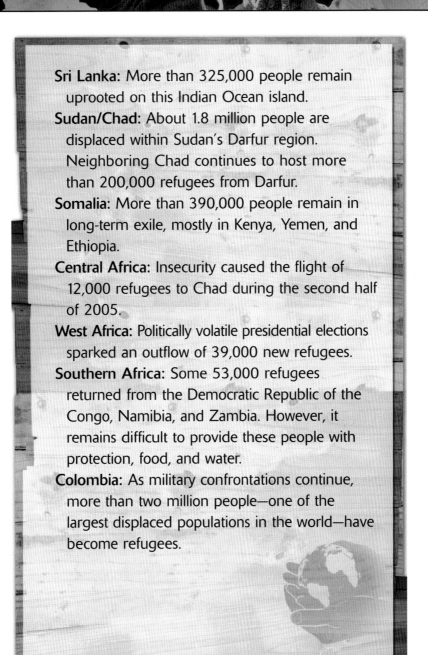

Sri Lanka: More than 325,000 people remain uprooted on this Indian Ocean island.

Sudan/Chad: About 1.8 million people are displaced within Sudan's Darfur region. Neighboring Chad continues to host more than 200,000 refugees from Darfur.

Somalia: More than 390,000 people remain in long-term exile, mostly in Kenya, Yemen, and Ethiopia.

Central Africa: Insecurity caused the flight of 12,000 refugees to Chad during the second half of 2005.

West Africa: Politically volatile presidential elections sparked an outflow of 39,000 new refugees.

Southern Africa: Some 53,000 refugees returned from the Democratic Republic of the Congo, Namibia, and Zambia. However, it remains difficult to provide these people with protection, food, and water.

Colombia: As military confrontations continue, more than two million people—one of the largest displaced populations in the world—have become refugees.

After meeting with officials from the agency, Jolie decided to learn more by going to the affected countries. She wanted to see for herself what refugee camps were like and how they helped people in need.

A Better Understanding Leads to Action

In February 2001, UNHCR invited Jolie to join a contingent of field workers on an eighteen-day mission to a number of refugee camps in Sierra Leone and Tanzania.

Jolie kept journals of her first several missions. (In 2003, they were published as *Notes from My Travels: Visits with Refugees in Africa, Cambodia, Pakistan, and Ecuador.*) She wrote about how she prepared for the trip and her interest in wanting to make a difference. "I have done a lot of research and talked with many people in Washington, D.C. I have read as much as I could. I have discovered statistics that shocked me and stories that broke my heart. I also read many things that made me sick." She continued, "I don't understand why some things are talked about and others are not. I don't know why I think I can make a difference. All I know is that I want to."

According to UNHCR, women, children, and the elderly comprise 80 percent of a typical refugee population. Here, a young girl stands by the tent she calls home at a makeshift refugee camp in Pakistan.

Jolie visited refugee camps in both nations. Refugee camps, which are essentially tent cities, can house anywhere from 200 to 800,000 people. They are temporary sites built by a government or governmental organization, like UNHCR, to assist people who have left their homeland to seek sanctuary in another country. Most refugees flee their home countries in fear of being persecuted for their religious beliefs, race, nationality, political opinion, or member-ship in a particular group (such as a tribe). The camps are designed to provide a safe haven for these people.

Camps provide refugees with food, medical aid, and a place to live. Oftentimes, refugee children receive some level of education. Education is not a priority, however, and when it is available, only younger children are taught.

The first camp Jolie visited was in Sierra Leone, a small nation located in western Africa. Sierra Leone had been devastated by years of brutal civil war, finally emerging from the conflict in 2002 with help from Great Britain and a large UN peacekeeping mission. Now, however, the nation of more than 5.3 million people is facing the challenge of reconstruction.

A young refugee from Sierra Leone carries water at the Kolahun refugee camp in Liberia.

Jolie witnessed firsthand the enormous challenges that refugees face. She saw an amputee camp filled with refugees who had lost limbs in the war. The visit made Jolie take stock of her own life and the opportunities she had been given.

"I was very focused on myself, on my career, on my life. We have so much and we want for other things and we don't realize how grateful we should be about things," Jolie told CNN news anchor Anderson Cooper in a 2006 interview to promote World Refugee Day. "And then, suddenly you see these people who are really fighting for something, who are really surviving, who have so much pain and loss and things that you have no idea. And you just feel like, your whole life, you have just been so sheltered and so spoiled with so much."

By the time Jolie boarded a plane to return to the United States, she knew that she would commit herself to helping refugees in some way.

Her Most Inspired Role

Jolie continued to travel the world to learn more about refugees. Over the course of seven months in 2001, Jolie visited other refugee camps. She took no press with her, and no one was there to capture photographs of her or to follow her like they do in Hollywood. There were no photos of her with refugees and aid workers in tabloids or newspapers. She told *Newsweek* magazine that she wanted to have the opportunity to educate herself fully before she spoke with any authority on the subject of refugees. "I saw that so many times the picture comes before the knowledge and the substance and I didn't want to do that to myself or to the organization," Jolie said.

For several months she visited different refugee camps, many in nations like Pakistan, a country aiding Afghan refugees. There she gained an understanding of UNHCR's role, what the refugees' struggles are, and what their living conditions at the camps are like. She also visited Tanzania and Cambodia.

"There were many things I hadn't been taught in school and daily events I was not hearing about in the news. I wanted to understand," Jolie said in an interview with *National Geographic*. "I believe in what the UN has always stood for—equality and the protection of human rights for all people. When I read about the twenty million people under the care of UNHCR I wanted to understand how in this day and age that many people could be displaced."

In August 2001, UNHCR named Angelina Jolie a Goodwill Ambassador at the organization's headquarters in Geneva, Switzerland. Ruud Lubbers, then the United Nations High Commissioner for Refugees, gave Jolie the honorary title. "We are very pleased that Ms. Jolie has generously agreed to give her time and energy to support UNHCR's work," Lubbers said. "She can help give a voice to refugees, many of whom live in the shadows of forgotten tragedies."

By becoming a Goodwill Ambassador, Jolie accepted the responsibility of meeting with and advocating for the protection of refugees on five continents. In her speech at

Jolie holds up her United Nations passport during the August 27, 2001, ceremony in which she was named a Goodwill Ambassador for the UNHCR.

About Goodwill Ambassadors

UNHCR's Goodwill Ambassadors are celebrities who use their talent and fame to advocate for refugees. Goodwill Ambassadors travel the world to help field workers at refugee camps. They also bring the important issues of refugee rights, poverty, and education to the media, where the causes can gain international attention. UNHCR first worked with Goodwill Ambassadors in the early 1980s, when British film actors Richard Burton and James Mason helped bring global attention to the agency.

Jolie is just one of eight Goodwill Ambassadors who currently work with UNHCR. The others, who represent countries all over the world, are also artists:

- **Barbara Hendricks**, world-renowned American opera singer (named an ambassador in 1987)
- **Adel Imam**, popular Egyptian actor (2000)
- **Giorgio Armani**, famous Italian fashion designer (2002)
- **Julien Clerc**, French singer (2003)
- **George Dalaras**, well-known contemporary Greek singer (2006)
- **Osvaldo Laport**, Latin American actor (2006)
- **Muazzez Ersoy**, popular Turkish singer (2007)

the ceremony, Jolie spoke of wanting to help those in need and being proactive about getting involved. "We cannot close ourselves off to information and ignore the fact that millions of people are out there suffering. I honestly want to help. I don't believe I feel differently from other people," Jolie said. "I think we all want justice and equality, a chance for a life with meaning. All of us would like to believe that if we were in a bad situation someone would help us."

During her first three years as a Goodwill Ambassador, Jolie concentrated her efforts on field missions, understanding the conflicts that caused people to flee their home nations, and visiting refugees and internally displaced persons all around the world.

CHAPTER TWO

Angelina's Fight to Help Refugees

By most accounts, it's rare for a Goodwill Ambassador to spend a month in a refugee camp. But Angelina Jolie wanted to be hands-on and forge her own experience. She knew that visiting the refugee camps would give her a perspective and insight that nothing else could.

Jolie's field visits as Goodwill Ambassador expanded her knowledge of the harrowing situations from which refugees had escaped, as well as the bleak conditions they faced in camps. Jolie saw that refugees' greatest needs were protection, and safety and education for their children. She also learned more about World Refugee Day

On June 20, 2007, thousands of people demonstrated in front of Notre Dame cathedral in Paris, France, to mark World Refugee Day.

and saw an outlet where she could use her celebrity status to capture the world's attention and focus it squarely on refugees and their struggles.

A New Life in a Strange Land

Starting over in another country is not easy. But for the more than thirty-five million people who have been forced to leave their homelands, it is the only way for them to survive. Approximately twelve million people currently live in refugee camps around the world.

In an interview with *National Geographic*, Jolie described the conditions of refugee camps. "Some of the camps have hundreds of thousands of people in horrible living conditions," Jolie told the magazine.

"One of the biggest problems is food distribution. Food is distributed in the camps every two weeks, but sometimes due to funding levels, food rations are cut. In some camps people are living on rations that provide only 60 to 80 percent of their daily nutritional needs."

In many camps, shelters are made from mud and twigs found in the bush, areas of tall grass and trees. When there are heavy rains, the huts collapse. Disease spreads easily and quickly among the refugees, and there is little medicine for those who get sick.

UNHCR strives to give refugees as much shelter, food and water, medical care, and schooling for children as possible. The organization also works to make sure that nations are aware of, and act on, their obligations to assist and protect refugees.

As a Goodwill Ambassador, Jolie has traveled to more than twenty countries on field missions with UNHCR workers. It was at camps around the world where Jolie saw the very real effects of war and violence on refugees. She also heard tales of escape and survival against all odds. One of Jolie's early field visits was to Ibarra, one of the largest refugee reception centers located in Ecuador. Jolie met several families who had fled violent conditions. Some families told her of loved ones who had been killed when their villages were attacked. Others told her how they escaped kidnapping and murder attempts, leaving everything they owned behind. Many saw their homes and villages destroyed.

"People's lives are truly in danger—not just in the sense that you feel your town is unsafe—their lives are actually being threatened and their houses are being burnt down," Jolie wrote in her journal, later published in *Notes from My Travels*.

In March 2003, Jolie embarked on a six-day field mission to Tanzania, her second to the country. She traveled to the western border camps for a firsthand look at UNHCR's operations in the area. She followed a group of ninety-one children who had just arrived from the Democratic Republic of the Congo, seeing them through their registration at Kigoma town. She then accompanied them on a bumpy ride to the Lugufu refugee camp, where they received relief items, such as clothing and medicine. These children had been separated from their families and had no way of finding their parents or grandparents. Jolie

While visiting the Lugufu camp in Tanzania in 2003, Jolie helped refugees and aid workers with the children arriving at the camp. These children were unaccompanied, having lost their parents and other family members.

helped the children build the huts in which they would live. Later, she joined the children as the camp's staff explained how the camp worked, and about its routine and activities.

Traveling to the town of Tine, Chad, a major point of entry for Darfur refugees, in June 2004, Jolie spoke to some Sudanese refugees in makeshift shelters. They told her of how they had fled their villages during attacks and how many of the women walked for several days with their children in search of safety. During this field mission, Jolie assisted aid workers in helping to board refugees into trucks that would take them to a safer refugee camp. To sustain them for the four-hour journey, she helped distribute high-protein biscuits to the women and children. The next day, Jolie joined a nutrition team from the Centers for Disease Control and Prevention (CDC) as they weighed and measured refugee children to check for malnourishment.

In August 2007, Jolie traveled to Iraq. She wanted to see the Iraq War's effects on the Iraqi people who have been forced to flee their homes due to the country's increasing violence. At Al Waleed, a makeshift refugee camp inside Iraq, Jolie walked among the tattered tents in an area where there is no running water or electricity, and no relief from the intense desert sun. She spent time with sick children and elderly refugees, who are suffering and dying from diseases like malaria and tuberculosis. These illnesses would be treatable if the camp had access to medicines and vaccines. She also inspected a site where UNHCR is building a school for the children among the 1,300 refugees.

On a visit to Iraq in 2007, Jolie meets an elderly woman at a refugee camp. The woman is one of more than four million people who have been uprooted by the war in Iraq.

A Timeline of Angelina Jolie's Field Missions

Angelina Jolie expects no special treatment when she travels on field missions. She lives in the same conditions as her fellow field workers and covers all of her own expenses. Jolie has traveled to more than twenty countries since 2001:

- **August 2007**: Iraq and Syria
- **February 2007**: Chad
- **December 2006**: Costa Rica
- **November 2006**: India
- **November 2005**: Pakistan
- **May 2005**: Pakistan
- **December 2004**: Lebanon
- **October 2004**: Sudan and Thailand
- **June 2004**: Chad
- **April 2004**: Arizona
- **December 2003**: Egypt and Jordan
- **August 2003**: Russian Federation
- **April 2003**: Sri Lanka
- **March 2003**: United Republic of Tanzania
- **December 2002**: Kosovo province of Serbia and Montenegro
- **October 2002**: Kenya
- **June 2002**: Ecuador
- **May 2002**: Thailand
- **March 2002**: Namibia
- **August 2001**: Pakistan
- **June–July 2001**: Cambodia
- **February 2001**: Sierra Leone

Assisting the World's Children

While life in the camps is strenuous for adults, children have just as difficult a time. Many children have lost one or both parents to violence, have very little food, and sometimes also have little to no clothing.

"The trauma children face as a result of being uprooted from their homes, often very suddenly, is devastating, and affects the rest of their lives," Jolie

These young children lie on the ground at the Otach camp in Darfur, a region of Sudan, Africa. Darfur is suffering through a civil war. Thousands of the region's people are refugees seeking help.

told *National Geographic*. "The very young children still have dreams. But the young teens have very little hope."

While in their villages, many children may have been able to go to school. But in the camps they must take care of younger siblings or spend their time gathering wood, collecting water, or doing the cooking. Oftentimes, the boys are the primary breadwinners for their families.

Educating Refugee Children

Jolie learned very quickly that in the refugee camps, children receive little to no education. Attending school is seen as a luxury when refugees struggle to have shelter and enough food and water.

Jolie and UNHCR are working to increase education in refugee camps. Jolie became active with schools and promoted UNHCR's education materials. She served as the honorary patron of the annual World Refugee Day school poster contest. She also joined former U.S. president Bill Clinton at the Clinton Global Initiative. The initiative is an endeavor of the William J. Clinton Foundation to strengthen the capacity of people in the United States and

Many refugee camps lack educational materials for the school-aged children who live there. UNHCR provides books and teaching supplies so children can continue their educations.

throughout the world to meet the challenges of global interdependence. Launched in 2005, the initiative is a nonpartisan means for action. Through an annual meeting, it brings together a community of global leaders to create and carry out innovative solutions for the world's most pressing global challenges.

Jolie has supported the initiative's efforts in raising $220 million for refugee education. The program will increase the access to education and educational materials for nine million refugee children worldwide by 2010. Resources will be provided to develop children's full potential. The program will emphasize girls' participation and will include activities like life-skills training, sport programs, disease prevention, and access to technology.

Jolie also cochairs the Education Partnership for Children of Conflict, founded by the Clinton Global Initiative. The partnership helps fund education programs for children affected by conflict.

Swedish Teens Raise Money for Refugee Children

Jolie has also supported other countries' efforts to help refugee children gain access to educational materials. Each year, for example, the Swedish Student Organization funds an educational project in a developing country. In 2006, nearly 80,000 Swedish teenagers from more than 250 schools participated in the "Operation a Day's Work" campaign. They raised more than $750,000 by selling homemade cookies and lemonade, and holding impromptu concerts in the streets. The money they raised went to Congolese refugee children living in

Rwanda's Gihembe camp. The money was used to refurbish classrooms, buy school materials, and train more teachers.

Jolie thanked the students for their generosity in an open letter, which was widely printed throughout Sweden's local and national newspapers.

World Refugee Day

Every year since 2000, on June 20, the world has celebrated World Refugee Day. Established by the United Nations General Assembly, World Refugee Day recognizes and celebrates the contribution of refugees throughout the world. It also helps to raise awareness of refugees and their struggles.

Jolie learned firsthand how hard it is for refugees' stories to be told. While on a field visit in Sierra Leone, Africa, a photographer arrived at the UNHCR office looking for information on the areas in conflict. Jolie told of his efforts in her journal. "[The photographer] was trying to help bring awareness so people could see what is happening and judge for themselves how they feel. I am sure that most of the pictures he takes are images many of us don't want to see—but should," she wrote. "He asked me where I was from. 'America.' 'Ah! I have been a photographer for ten years. American press don't buy these kinds of pictures. Other countries do.'"

This interaction fueled Jolie's interest in increasing refugee awareness in countries around the world, including the United States. She began attending World Refugee Day events in 2002. Since then, she has played a major role in promoting the event and raising awareness. In 2004, Jolie launched a three-day series of events in Washington, D.C., with UNHCR and then secretary of state Colin Powell. The year's theme was "To Feel at Home." Just days earlier, Jolie had returned from visiting emergency operations in Chad, where she assisted in transporting 160,000 Sudanese refugees who had fled violence in their country.

Jolie donated $500,000 to UNHCR to establish the National Legal Resource Center, which works with the Office of Refugee Resettlement. The resource center provides lawyer services to child refugees who arrive alone in the United States.

In 2005, Jolie again launched World Refugee Day, this time with U.S. secretary of state Condoleezza Rice and Paul Rusesabagina. Rusesabagina is a hotel manager who provided protection to refugees fleeing the 1994 genocide in Rwanda. He turned the luxury hotel where he worked into a refugee camp, helping to keep thousands of people alive during the fighting. Rusesabagina's story was the subject of the Oscar-nominated film *Hotel Rwanda*.

In 2006, Jolie again lent her celebrity to the cause and filmed a thirty-second TV commercial urging people not to forget about refugees. The message was broadcast around the world. That year, Jolie also gave an exclusive interview to CNN's Anderson Cooper. The interview was shown on Anderson's news show, *Anderson Cooper 360°*, and aired on CNN in the United States and on CNN International. The program reached more than two hundred countries and territories around the world.

Jolie and U.S. secretary of state Condoleezza Rice attend the launching ceremony for World Refugee Day in 2005. Founded by UNHCR, World Refugee Day is held annually on June 20.

During the interview, Jolie talked about her experiences as a Goodwill Ambassador, the camps she has visited, and some of the stories of the thousands of refugees she has met along the way. She also stressed the need for the world to come together and help the nations that need assistance. Cooper asked Jolie if she felt she made a difference, and if she sees change from her efforts. "I do," Jolie responded. "I can see people who say, 'We really need a well.' And I can go back one year later and see it built."

Honored for Her Work

Since beginning her worldwide mission to advocate for refugees, Jolie has been honored by a number of agencies for her passion and commitment. In October 2003, she was the first recipient of the Citizen of the World Award from the United Nations Correspondents Association, an agency of more than two hundred journalists from dozens of countries representing hundreds of publications and broad-casters around the world. The organization's awards recognize and encourage excellence in the worldwide reporting of the United Nations and its affiliated agencies and the work they strive to accomplish.

"[This award] means that I have done good by an organization that I care a great deal about and that I didn't let them down, that I represented them properly and that they're happy with that," she said at the ceremony. "And it means that, if I die tomorrow, I can leave my son something that says I did something good with my life."

Jolie has also received the Global Humanitarian Award, given to her in October 2005 by the United Nations Association of the United States of America (UNA-USA). The president of UNA-USA, William Luers, described Jolie as a person who stands apart from other celebrities involved in humanitarian work. "She has gone to the refugee camps. She has sat with heads of state. She has personally and publicly engaged in ways to better manage the problems surrounding this noble cause," he said.

In June 2007, Jolie's nomination for membership on the Council on Foreign Relations was approved. The council is a prestigious think tank, a group that conducts research and advocates for policy change.

Above, on October 11, 2005, Jolie accepts the Global Humanitarian Award from John Whitehead, the vice chairman of the United Nations Association of the United States of America (UNA-USA). She dedicated the award to the refugees she helps.

She joins a number of influential people on the council, including former presidents Bill Clinton and Jimmy Carter, Secretary of State Condoleezza Rice, and journalists Diane Sawyer and Tom Brokaw. The group represents a generation of policy leaders striving to influence change.

CHAPTER THREE

Angelina's Support to Additional Humanitarian Causes

As Angelina Jolie traveled the world in support of refugees' rights, she became keenly aware of the many other problems that were directly and indirectly related to refugees. Among them were poverty in third world nations, land mines in Cambodia, and the conflict occurring in Darfur.

Jolie has supported each of these causes in her role as a Goodwill Ambassador, raising awareness of the problems, often donating her time and money, and inspiring people to take a more active role not only in understanding the issues but in helping to provide support for their solutions.

Poverty in Third World Nations

As a result of seeing the effects of poverty so intimately, Jolie began to get involved in the United Nations' Millennium Promise program. The program is part of the United Nations' Millennium Project, which works to recommend a concrete plan for reversing poverty, hunger, and disease around the world. In 2000, the project launched the Millennium Development Goals, consisting of the following eight objectives:

- *Eradicate extreme poverty and hunger*
- *Achieve universal primary education*
- *Promote gender equality and empower women*
- *Reduce child mortality*
- *Improve maternal health*
- *Combat HIV/AIDS, malaria, and other diseases*
- *Ensure environmental stability*
- *Develop a global partnership for development*

The mission of the Millennium Promise, which was adopted by more than two hundred world leaders, is to achieve these eight goals, hopefully by 2015. Doing so will permanently improve the lives of millions of people.

OmniPeace Supports the Millennium Project

After getting involved in the Millennium Project, Jolie also joined OmniPeace. This organization's

Women living in Sauri, Kenya, the first Millennium Village funded by Columbia University's Earth Institute, prepare the land for planting. Maize will be grown and harvested to feed the entire village.

vision is to address vital humanitarian needs through the distribution and sale of consumer products. The products range from T-shirts and tank tops to tote bags and baseball caps. They are sold around the world to raise awareness of extreme poverty in sub-Saharan Africa and provide financial support. Fifty percent of the proceeds are donated to Millennium Promise.

Jolie has regularly been seen wearing an OmniPeace T-shirt, as have many other popular actors, actresses, and performers. OmniPeace has donated thousands of dollars in support of Millennium Promise.

Inspiring Young People to Action

In addition to its eight goals, the Millennium Promise established Millennium Villages, rural African communities that are given resources to help lift themselves out of extreme poverty. To bring attention to the Millennium Villages, and inspire young people to get involved, Jolie partnered with MTV and filmed a documentary on poverty in Africa.

MTV may be well known as the place to go for the latest music videos, reality shows, and current news on artists, but the channel has also been reaching out to its young audience through groundbreaking documentaries and television series that highlight important issues like drug abuse, the environment, and AIDS.

In 2005, MTV followed Angelina Jolie as she joined Dr. Jeffrey Sachs on a trip to Sauri, a Millennium Village in Kenya, Africa, to see the progress the village has made in the five years since the program began.

Sachs is the world's foremost expert on extreme poverty. He is the director of the Earth Institute at Columbia University in New York City, as well as a professor of health policy and management. From 2002 to 2006, he was the director of the UN Millennium Project and served as a special adviser to United Nations secretary-general Kofi Annan. Sachs is also the president and cofounder of Millennium Promise Alliance, a nonprofit organization that works with the Millennium Project.

The Diary of Angelina Jolie and Dr. Jeffrey Sachs in Africa showed Jolie and Sachs as they visited Sauri. The Millennium Project provided the village with simple, greatly needed everyday items, such as bed nets to keep away malaria-carrying mosquitoes, fertilizer to grow crops, school lunches so every child was assured at least one meal a day, school equipment, and medicine for people living with HIV and AIDS.

Jolie was in Sauri on the day the school received its first computer. "The first time they saw the computer they weren't that excited," Jolie said. "Then I realized, of course they're not, because to them it

Dr. Jeffrey Sachs *(center)*, director of the Earth Institute at Columbia University, stands in a field in a Millennium Village in Malawi, Africa.

was a weird box." Sachs brought the computer, donated by Columbia University, to the village. He connected the computer to the Internet and assisted a young student named Paul in writing an e-mail to the secretary-general of the United Nations. Just a few minutes later, a reply arrived from the UN, congratulating the village on the success it had experienced to date.

"This is not emergency relief," Sachs told *Good Morning America* in an interview to promote the MTV special. "This is an opportunity to solve poverty once and for all. It's not charity. It's an investment, an investment that could help make the world a safer place."

The TV special's airdate, September 14, 2005, coincided with the opening of the UN Summit on the Millennium Development Goals. Jolie, Sachs, MTV, and the UN all hope the documentary has helped young people to understand what poverty in Africa means, and they hope it will inspire action.

"We are at a unique threshold in human history, where the crisis we face in Africa is matched only by our degree of hope that we can and will be a force for change," Jolie said in a statement. "I'm certain

Millennium Villages

In addition to its eight goals, the Millennium Project established Millennium Villages Sub-Sahara Africa. In ten African countries (Ethiopia, Ghana, Kenya, Malawi, Mali, Nigeria, Rwanda, Senegal, Tanzania, and Uganda), there are twelve clusters of villages. Each is located in distinct agricultural and ecological zones—arid or humid, highland or lowland, grain producing or pastoral—that reflect the range of farming, water, disease, and infrastructure challenges facing Africa. Every village's strategies are tailored to its specific location so that refugees living in the area can learn how to use their natural resources to their advantage. The twelve villages are located in:

- Koraro, Ethiopia
- Bonsaaso, Ghana
- Dertu, Kenya
- Sauri, Kenya
- Mwandama, Malawi
- Tiby, Mali
- Ikaram, Nigeria
- Pampaida, Nigeria
- Mayange, Rwanda
- Potou, Senegal
- Mbola, Tanzania
- Ruhiira, Uganda

the stories in this special will inspire viewers the same way these experiences inspired me, and I'm hopeful that increased awareness of the issues in Africa will bring about a new wave of progress and activism among young people everywhere."

Land Mines in Cambodia

Jolie was stunned when she first learned of the land-mine situation in Cambodia during the filming of *Lara Croft: Tomb Raider*. She couldn't believe the land was littered with mines that killed or caused severe injury to thousands of adults and children. Many times, while filming, Jolie was scared she might be in danger. "I went off into certain areas where you were told that nothing had exploded, therefore it was not considered a high-risk area," she said in an interview with the *Journal of Mine Action*, a publication of the Mine Action Information Center at Virginia's James Madison University. "You, along with everybody else, stay on a very clear path that has already been walked. You don't stray from it."

Jolie had the opportunity to detonate a land mine with the HALO Trust, an organization that works around the world to clear land mines from various

A man trains to clear land mines in a practice field in Cambodia. The country contains an untold number of mines as a result of civil war. Each year, thousands of Cambodians are injured or killed by the mines.

countries. Joining them in Cambodia, Jolie was with the organization when they located land mines. At the end of each day, the organization detonated a mine. "It was a great experience," Jolie says of exploding a land mine. "If HALO hadn't been there and [they] weren't detonating [them], [the mines] might otherwise be hurting someone. It was a great feeling."

UNHCR has been working with de-miners like HALO in nations such as Afghanistan and Namibia where land mines are a problem. Jolie also has been working with the International Campaign to Ban Landmines, an organization that raises awareness of the dangers of land mines.

Conflict in Darfur

During her world travels, Jolie visited the African country of Sudan, a remote desert nation involved in a brutal civil war. Darfur is a region in Sudan.

The conflict in Darfur is complex. Problems began in February 2003, when decades of drought, desertification, and overpopulation caused people to move around in search of food and water for themselves and their livestock. As they searched, they began to occupy land that did not belong to

them, causing conflict among
the many tribes of Sudan. This
resulted in a massive civil war
and genocide, which is deliberate
killing of an ethnic, religious, or
national group. Thousands of
people died. Thousands more
became refugees, fleeing attack-
ing tribes and seeking safety in
bordering nations like Chad.

Jolie has visited the region
of Darfur on three separate
occasions. She has used her
understanding of the conflict
and her status as a Goodwill
Ambassador to raise worldwide
awareness of the situation. In
April 2006, for example, Jolie
took out a full-page advertisement
in *USA Today*. "I chose to take

At a refugee camp in Darfur, Sudan, Jolie talks
to a group of children about their experiences.
During her 2004 visit to the region, Jolie also
toured destroyed villages and met with victims
of the violence.

out this ad because when Congress returns from recess they have the chance to fully fund peace-keepers in Darfur," Jolie told *People* magazine. "The situation in Darfur has been going on for too long. It's only getting worse. Reports are pouring in about mass atrocities including children getting raped and killed. If people are aware of the facts, I believe many will be driven to action."

Less than a year later, Jolie made another public statement in support of Darfur. On February 28, 2007, the *Washington Post* ran an op-ed article written by Jolie. The piece, entitled "Justice for Darfur," sought to promote enduring peace in Sudan and called for the prosecution of those committing crimes against humanity. "As the prosecutions unfold, I hope the international community will intervene, right away, to protect the people of Darfur and prevent further violence," Jolie wrote. "The refugees don't need more resolutions or statements of concern. They need follow-through on past promises of action." In the article, Jolie wrote that she had visited these refugee camps before, and when back again, found herself hearing the same stories of fear and death, and seeing the same lack of clean water, medicine, and

The Sudanese children pictured above collect rainwater for their refugee camp. The water will be purified and then used for drinking and cooking.

security. There has been no improvement in the refugees' quality of life.

UNHCR estimates that nearly 1.6 million people have been displaced in the three provinces of Darfur, and more than 200,000 have fled to the neighboring nation of Chad. "It has become clear to me that there will be no enduring peace without justice," Jolie wrote. "History shows that there will be another Darfur, another exodus, in a vicious cycle of bloodshed and retribution. But an international court finally exists. It will be as strong as the support we give it. This might be the moment we stop the cycle of violence and end our tolerance for crimes against humanity."

CHAPTER FOUR

Angelina the Lobbyist

As she visited refugee camps in a number of third world nations, Angelina Jolie learned early on that while her field missions gave her insight into the living conditions and situations of displaced people, there was another role she would have to assume in order to gain support for refugees. She would need to become a lobbyist.

"As much as I would love to never visit Washington, that's the way to move the ball," Jolie said in an interview with *Forbes* magazine. She headed to Washington, D.C., to begin lobbying. Jolie soon found that her lobbyist role would take her around the world and that she would have the opportunity to meet with government leaders and influence nations beyond the United States. She began meeting with government officials to advocate for their greater support. In addition, she called on business and political leaders to use their influence to keep refugee issues at the top of the international agenda. Jolie also met with more than twenty representatives in the United States Congress and Senate to influence support for refugees and for UNHCR and other organizations.

World Economic Forum and the Council of Business Leaders

Held annually in Davos, Switzerland, the World Economic Forum is an independent, international organization committed to improving the state of the world. The forum is a week of discussions, lectures, and workshops where artists, academics, religious leaders, and campaigners from organizations like UNHCR join business leaders and politicians.

At the January 2005 forum, UNHCR's deputy high commissioner, Wendy Chamberlin, announced the formation of the Council of Business Leaders, a

Jolie and her partner, actor Brad Pitt, are photographed with UN secretary-general Kofi Annan and his wife, Nane, at the 2006 World Economic Forum in Davos, Switzerland. The annual forum brings together leaders from around the world.

program intended to boost UNHCR's efforts to address the plight of innocent people who are forced to flee their homes. The council's initiative is to rally corporate support and boost private-sector involvement in refugee work. The 2005 forum occurred just days after a devastating tsunami destroyed many areas of Southeast Asia, killing thousands of people and leaving thousands more homeless. Speaking at the forum, Jolie took the opportunity to motivate nations around the world to continue to build on the energy and spirit of humanity that resulted after the tsunami.

"If there's been one positive thing to come out of the immense tragedy of the tsunami, it is the amazing response by people and organizations across the world," Jolie told the audience. "What we need now is for this momentum, and this generosity, to be translated into a sustained effort to help solve some of the world's other neglected crises, like the desperate situation in Chad and Sudan."

The council consists of executives from five major corporations—Merck and Co., Inc.; Nike, Inc.; Nestlé; PricewaterhouseCoopers; and Microsoft Corporation—that are working with UNHCR to improve opportunities for refugees. Together, these companies will advise UNHCR on strategies to create innovative public-private partnerships. They will also help the agency find new sources of private-sector funding to complement the voluntary contributions from governments, which often cover only basic needs.

Jolie encouraged the companies to get involved and help make change possible. "Refugees don't have the luxury of choice," she said. "They flee to save their lives. They are confronted with the toughest possible decision—to leave behind everything they have and everything they know—because of factors out of their control. It's up to all of us to help them. Right now, so many of them get so little help from so few of us—and that is something we can choose to change. It's not even that tough a choice."

The Unaccompanied Child Protection Act

Each year, more than five thousand children from around the world arrive in the United States unaccompanied by adults, their families either killed or missing. Jolie heard many heartbreaking stories during an official UNHCR visit to Phoenix, Arizona, where she visited the Southwest Key Program. The Southwest Key Program, a shelter for unaccompanied children seeking assistance, has become one of the United States' largest care providers for unaccompanied immigrant children. It offers housing, education, counseling, recreation, and medical services. Case workers are also available to help resolve children's legal issues with immigration. The organization operates forty programs in seven states and helps thousands of young people every day.

The Council of Business Leaders:
UNHCR's Corporate Partners

According to the UNHCR Web site, the Council of Business Leaders meets four times a year. Its role is to "catalyze innovative public-private partnerships; explore synergies among UNHCR's corporate partners through joint investments; bring key resources to the forefront, such as knowledge, expertise, access, and reach; conduct outreach and build networks to assist UNHCR in maximizing sources of financial and other support; champion UNHCR within the corporation and in the external business community; and raise public awareness of UNHCR and draw attention to the refugee cause."

In working toward these goals, some of the member corporations' accomplishments include:

- **Merck and Co., Inc.:** This leading pharmaceutical company has helped UNHCR and the International Council of Nurses to introduce the Mobile Health Libraries program, which benefits both communities and refugee camps in Tanzania.
- **Microsoft Corporation:** The computer and software giant and UNHCR have worked in partnership for many years. Together they have developed solutions to register and reunite refugees, supported retraining programs, and

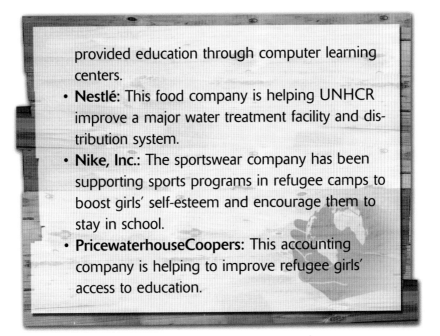

provided education through computer learning centers.

- **Nestlé:** This food company is helping UNHCR improve a major water treatment facility and distribution system.
- **Nike, Inc.:** The sportswear company has been supporting sports programs in refugee camps to boost girls' self-esteem and encourage them to stay in school.
- **PricewaterhouseCoopers:** This accounting company is helping to improve refugee girls' access to education.

Jolie was moved by the thousands of children who had not only survived the often harrowing situations that brought them to the United States but were trying to weave their way through a complicated immigration system. After her visit to the Southwest Key Program, Jolie met with senior government officials in Washington, D.C. She then took a key role in building awareness and support for the Unaccompanied Alien Child Protection Act of 2003, a Congressional bill cosponsored by U.S. senators

Jolie speaks at a June 19, 2003, news conference for the Unaccompanied Child Protection Act of 2003. Senators Sam Brownback *(left)* and Dianne Feinstein *(right)* sponsored the bill.

Dianne Feinstein and Sam Brownback. In addition to raising tremendous public support for the bill, during private meetings with Jolie, senators Arlen Specter and Hillary Rodham Clinton, the former first lady, agreed to cosponsor it. The bill was designed to ensure that unaccompanied children would be treated properly and humanely while in custody, and that they would also be assigned legal counsel and/or guardians to assist them with immigration proceedings.

"When children cross into this country alone, they are scared, we must hear them out before we make the choice to either allow them asylum in our country or send them away," Jolie said about the bill. "It is unethical to not listen to these children. Without legal representation we are sending children to court to represent themselves in a language that most of them don't understand."

On March 8, 2005, Jolie took part in a National Press Club luncheon in Washington, D.C., where she promoted the Unaccompanied Alien Child Protection Act of 2003 and also announced the founding of the National Center for Refugee and Immigrant Children. The center was established with a $500,000 donation from Jolie. The mission of the organization is to provide free legal advice and social services for unaccompanied immigrant children as they navigate the U.S. immigration courts. These children, often fleeing domestic abuse, gang violence, trafficking, or poverty, arrive in the United States without parents or resources. Sometimes they are deported without having ever spoken to an attorney. Some may be seeking asylum, others may simply want to reunite with family members or seek opportunities that are

Addressing the Washington, D.C., National Press Club luncheon on March 8, 2005, Jolie talks about her work to help assist immigrant children arriving in the United States.

not available to them in their home countries. The center ensures that these children receive the proper legal, social, and health services that they deserve. Since 2005, the center has worked with over 1,200 attorneys and 1,800 children from 33 different countries. To date, close to 650 children have been matched with lawyers across the country. The center recently received the Emil Gumpert Award from the American College of Trial Lawyers for its excellence in immigrant child advocacy.

Going to the Hill

Jolie spent considerable time lobbying for different bills. She met with representatives of the U.S. Senate and House of Representatives to urge them to adopt the cause of protecting children's rights. The first bill asked the United States to spend $500 million, and $15 billion over ten years, to educate children in the poorest regions of the world. Jolie worked with New York State senator and former first lady Hillary Rodham Clinton, who proposed the bill. The second bill provided legal help to alien minors who are alone and pass through U.S. borders. The Senate passed the bill in December 2005. However, it was stalled in the House of Representatives.

Her third bill, the Assistance for Orphans and Other Vulnerable Children in Developing Countries Act of 2005, authorizes U.S. support for a wide range of services and reforms to help millions of children in poor countries. It was signed by President George W. Bush in November 2005. Since the bill has been passed, Jolie has been fighting to find funding for it. She appeared back on Capitol Hill to ask for financial support. "We worked so hard to pass a bill, then you realize you have to figure out a way to pay for it," Jolie commented in an interview with *Forbes* magazine.

"By fully funding this legislation, we would be saying to the world that we believe that the life of a child in the poorest country is just as important,

With Senator Richard Lugar, Jolie speaks about the UN Millennium Development Goals and urges full funding of the Assistance for Orphans and Other Vulnerable Children in Developing Countries Act of 2005.

just as valuable, as the lives of the children in the United States," Jolie said in an interview with *People* magazine.

In all, Jolie has met with more than twenty different representatives from the U.S. House of Representatives and Senate. Her goal is to continue to lobby those in positions of leadership who can help her increase awareness for refugees and work to facilitate change from within the government.

CHAPTER FIVE

Angelina the Philanthropist

Angelina Jolie commands a hefty paycheck for her job as an actress. Reportedly, she earns around $15 million per movie. But Jolie sees her salary as just one more way she can help people less fortunate than her. The actress has been very forthcoming about her decision to give away one-third of her income in support of organizations that aid refugees around the world. "I have a stupid income for what I do for a living," Jolie told CNN's Anderson Cooper in an interview. Jolie contributes to organizations in a number of ways. Sometimes she contributes outright with a personal check. Other times, she goes through the foundation she established with her partner, actor Brad Pitt.

Pitt, one of Hollywood's most famous actors, has appeared in more than forty films. Like Jolie, he has been involved in charitable causes for a number of years. He has become a vocal ambassador for the One Campaign, which seeks to eliminate poverty. In addition, Pitt chairs the jury for the Global Green project. Global Green seeks to reduce climate change by constructing environmentally friendly buildings and cities. The project has been deeply involved in the reconstruction of homes in the New Orleans area that were destroyed in 2005 by Hurricane Katrina.

The Jolie-Pitt Foundation

In September 2006, Jolie and Pitt established a charitable foundation to help fund refugee-related causes. The foundation has donated millions of dollars to organizations around the world that place an emphasis on finding solutions to refugee-related problems.

"Angelina and Brad are committed to using their resources to help the world's most vulnerable people," said Trevor Neilson, their philanthropic adviser and spokesperson. To date, Jolie and Pitt have made a number of significant donations to groups around the world.

Global Action for Children

The Global Action for Children organization predicts that by 2010, the worldwide number of children orphaned by HIV/AIDS will exceed twenty million. Millions of other children will be vulnerable through the loss of caregivers, teachers, community leaders, and health care workers. The organization also estimates that eleven million children under the age of five die each year from preventable or treatable illnesses, such as diarrhea, pneumonia, malaria, and measles. Malnutrition is a factor in more than half of these cases. Global Action for Children raises money to support children in developing countries.

Jolie was on hand in April 2007 for the launch of the organization, and she spoke at a press conference. Through their foundation, Jolie and Pitt also donated $1 million to the organization. Jennifer Delaney, U.S. director for Global Action for Children, expressed her gratitude to the Jolie-Pitt Foundation for its contribution. "Angelina Jolie and Brad Pitt not only

Together with education and health leaders, Jolie *(far right)* and Rev. Mpho Tutu *(far left)* announce the launch of Global Action for Children on April 26, 2007.

care, but more important, are taking concrete action to address the fact that there will be twenty million children orphaned by AIDS by 2010, and millions more orphaned by tuberculosis, malaria, and conflict or whose parents are sick and dying," Delaney said.

Jolie and Pitt's involvement in the organization is also personal. On July 6, 2005, Jolie adopted a baby girl from Ethiopia. Zahara Marley Jolie-Pitt was left an orphan because of the AIDS epidemic in Africa.

When Jolie returned to the United States with Zahara, the child was hospitalized in a New York City–area hospital for more than a week. She was treated for dehydration and malnourishment. Global Action for Children is working to help children like Zahara by advocating for orphans and other vulnerable children in the developing world.

At the press conference, Jolie promoted the organization and spoke about her daughter. "Zahara was orphaned by AIDS, so I don't have to tell you how precious I think these children are," she said. "I am here to simply ask you to think about orphaned children not as a burden, but as an opportunity. Their education is an investment in our future. They have to work very, very hard to survive, but when they are given a chance, they grow strong."

Doctors Without Borders

Doctors Without Borders, or Médecins sans Frontières as it is known internationally, is an independent humanitarian organization that delivers medical and emergency aid in more than seventy countries to people affected by armed conflict, epidemics, and natural or man-made disasters. It also provides

Jolie and her partner Brad Pitt take their daughter Zahara, adopted from Ethiopia, and son Maddox, adopted from Cambodia, on a walk through Mumbai, the capital of India.

Angelina Jolie's Children

Angelina Jolie and her partner, Brad Pitt, are the parents of four children. They have adopted three children, all from countries where Jolie lends her support. They also have a biological daughter. Each of the children was born in a third world nation, and each has a unique story.

- **Maddox Chivan Jolie-Pitt**, born August 5, 2001, in Cambodia, was adopted by Jolie on March 10, 2002. While Jolie was filming *Lara Croft: Tomb Raider* in Cambodia, she spent time at an orphanage, where she met Maddox. The child, whose nickname is Mad, has spent the first several years of his life accompanying Jolie everywhere.
- **Zahara Marley Jolie-Pitt**, born January 8, 2005, is the second child adopted by Jolie. Zahara, or "Z" as she is called by her family, was orphaned by AIDS in Ethiopia, Africa's second most populated country. Jolie adopted Zahara on July 6, 2005. Pitt, who became part of Jolie's life in 2005, legally adopted Maddox and Zahara later that year.
- **Shiloh Nouvel Jolie-Pitt**, born May 27, 2006, is Jolie and Pitt's biological child. She was born in Namibia, a southern African nation. Shiloh's

birth was heavily reported in the media, and several magazines sought to purchase the first photos of the couple's baby. It has been reported that *People* paid more than $4 million to publish the pictures in its magazine, and the British magazine *Hello!* paid approximately $3.5 million to publish the images in its publication. The amount of money each magazine paid makes these photographs of Shiloh the most expensive celebrity images to date. Jolie and Pitt donated all of the profits from the photographs to an undisclosed charity.

- **Pax Thien Jolie-Pitt**, born in November 2003, was adopted by Jolie and Pitt in March 2007. Pax was born in Vietnam and had been living at the Tam Binh orphanage outside Ho Chi Minh City, the largest city in Vietnam. According to adoption officials, Pax was abandoned at a hospital as a baby.

After adopting Maddox from Cambodia and Zahara from Ethiopia, Jolie told *Good Morning America* that if she adopted again, it might be a good idea to "balance the races so there's another African person in the house for Z and another Asian person in the house for Mad."

assistance to those without access to health care. The Jolie-Pitt Foundation donated $1 million to the organization to help fund the delivery of medical aid to refugees.

"In the most troubled parts of the world—places that much of the world has abandoned—MSF is always there," said Jolie in a statement she issued about the Jolie-Pitt Foundation contribution. "I have seen these brave men and women working

A member of Doctors Without Borders provides water to a young refugee at the Kibumba Hutu refugee camp in Goma, Zaire, during the Rwandan genocide in 1994.

in war zones and horrific conditions and I deeply admire them."

As part of its work around the world, Doctors Without Borders has established massive vaccine campaigns to keep controllable illnesses like malaria, yellow fever, and meningitis from spreading. It also provides training and supervision of medical personnel, water and sanitation improvement, food and nutrition, and patient care for those who are ill, as well as data collection to keep track of the health of those living in crisis areas.

The Daniel Pearl Foundation

In January 2002, while living in Bombay, India, as a foreign correspondent for the *Wall Street Journal*, Daniel Pearl ventured into Pakistan to cover the war on terror. While investigating a story, Pearl was abducted. For weeks, heads of state, religious leaders, and people around the world fought for his release. Four weeks after his abduction, however, it was confirmed that the terrorists who had kidnapped Pearl had murdered him.

Pearl's family and friends formed the Daniel Pearl Foundation in part to address the root causes of the tragedy, in the spirit, style, and principles that shaped Pearl's work and character. According to the foundation's Web site, these principles include "uncompromised objectivity and integrity; insightful and unconventional perspective; tolerance and respect for people of all cultures; unshaken belief in the effectiveness of education and communication; and the love of music, humor, and friendship." On what would have been Pearl's forty-third birthday, the Jolie-Pitt Foundation made a $100,000 donation to the Daniel Pearl Foundation. Jolie and Pitt also forged a close friendship with Pearl's wife, Mariane. Five years after Pearl was murdered, Jolie portrayed Mariane Pearl in *A Mighty Heart*, a film based on Mariane's memoir about her husband's life as a journalist, his disappearance, and his murder.

Duk Lost Boys Clinic

In March 2007, the Jolie-Pitt Foundation donated $100,000 to assist in the construction of the Duk Lost Boys Clinic. John Bul Dau, the director of the Direct Change Sudan Project, founded the clinic. Dau was one of the four thousand "Lost Boys" of Sudan, a group of young orphaned boys. In 1987, when he was just thirteen years old, Dau was driven from his village and separated from his family during the civil war in southern Sudan. He spent years living in refugee camps in Ethiopia and Kenya before making his way to the United States in 2001.

Dau eventually made his way to Syracuse, New York, and became a spokesperson for the Lost Boys and Lost Girls of Sudan. He earned a degree in policy studies from Syracuse University and founded

Jolie visits with former Sudan refugee John Bul Dau after the premiere of *God Grew Tired of Us*, a film that Brad Pitt *(background)* produced. The film is based on Dau's memoir about his experiences.

the Duk Lost Boys Clinic, which is located in the village from which Dau initially fled as a child.

Dau wrote a book called *God Grew Tired of Us: A Memoir*, which tells the story of his refugee years. The book was the basis for a documentary also called *God Grew Tired of Us*, which follows the journey of three boys from Sudan, including their challenges adjusting to life in the United States. Pitt served as an executive producer of the film, which won the Grand Jury Prize and the Audience Award at the 2006 Sundance Film Festival.

Pitt and Jolie's donation helped to fund the final construction of a medical clinic and its ongoing operations. The clinic is the region's first modern medical facility. It is estimated that the clinic will serve more than 150,000 residents of Duk County.

Darfur

The Jolie-Pitt Foundation has also made a number of contributions to the region of Darfur. The couple donated a total of $1 million to UNHCR, the International Rescue Committee, and SOS Children's Villages, which provides psychological assistance to traumatized children. All three agencies are active in providing life-saving humanitarian assistance to the more than two million people displaced within Darfur and the 240,000 refugees from Darfur living in refugee camps in eastern Chad.

The Environment in Cambodia and the Maddox Jolie-Pitt Project

Jolie has built a long-standing relationship with the nation of Cambodia. Not only is it the place where she first began her journey toward humanitarian causes, it's also the birth nation of her oldest son, Maddox Chivan Jolie-Pitt. After adopting a child, fighting for the removal of land mines, and purchasing land and building a home in Cambodia, Jolie decided to establish a wildlife sanctuary in the northwestern province of Battambang, not far from where her son was born.

In 2002, Jolie established a program now known as the Maddox Jolie-Pitt Project (MJP), named for her son and designed to assist his native country. The MJP is a conservation and community development program to help protect the Samlaut area, including a key watershed park located on the border of

Cambodia and Thailand. The MJP's goals are to provide protection to the wildlife that lives within the Samlaut National Park and establish the park as a safe haven for the many endangered and internationally important species that are indigenous to Cambodia. The project provides patrols throughout the park to monitor the animals and keep hunters away. The project also conducts field surveys and documents the different types of animals living within the park.

In December 2005, Jolie reevaluated the objectives of the MJP and created a second initiative. In addition to wildlife conservation, the MJP now works to help alleviate poverty in the impoverished communities surrounding the park. The MJP is using the United Nations Millennium Development Goals as a framework for assisting these villages. The MJP provides the villages with education and health care. The villagers are also taught how to build structures and roads, enhance their cultural preservation, create sustainable farmland, and establish a spiritual center with youth groups for the villages' children. To date, to help them become self-sufficient, the MJP has provided more than twenty villages with seeds, cows, and fruit trees.

On July 2, 2005, with her son Maddox, Jolie attends Live 8, Africa Calling, in England. The free concert, one of ten held simultaneously around the world, raised awareness for the Make Poverty History global campaign.

As a result of her dedication and in recognition of her environmental and conservation work in the country, King Norodom Sihamoni gave Jolie Cambodian citizenship.

Maternity Wards in Namibia

After their biological daughter, Shiloh, was born in Namibia, Africa, Jolie and Pitt decided to donate $300,000 to state hospitals in two towns for maternity equipment. "We want to contribute to Namibia and the people who have been so gracious to us at this time," the couple said in a statement. Jolie, Pitt, Maddox, and Zahara arrived in the nation one month prior to Shiloh's birth and sought privacy. The nation was honored to welcome them, even offering Shiloh Namibian citizenship.

Using the Media to Highlight the Issues

Jolie has become adept at taking her mission to people around the world, raising awareness through any means she can.

As a well-known actress, Jolie gets a significant amount of media attention. Photographers and reporters follow her constantly, seeking a comment on her movies and her children. Jolie has worked to turn that media attention away from herself and onto the issues for which she advocates.

In February 2007, the *Washington Post* published a letter Jolie sent to the newspaper's op-ed page. The letter stressed the need for justice and increased involvement of the International Criminal Court to establish an enduring peace in Darfur. In the article, titled "Justice for Darfur," Jolie recalled meeting a teenage boy at a refugee camp in Chad. As she asked his fellow refugees what they wanted, he responded, "We want a trial." Jolie urged for increased justice for the region and to give the refugees what they wanted: a trial against their perpetrators.

The *Washington Post* op-ed piece was not Jolie's first published writing about her experiences. In 2003, Jolie's book, *Notes from My Travels: Visits with Refugees in Africa, Cambodia, Pakistan, and Ecuador,* was published. The book is a collection of Jolie's journal entries that chronicled her first field missions to refugee camps around the world.

The book's forward is written by Ruud Lubbers, the former United Nations High Commissioner for Refugees. In it, he praises Jolie for her work with his agency and for her dedication to refugees around the world. "Since her appointment as a Goodwill Ambassador, Angelina Jolie has more than fulfilled my expectations. She has proven to be a close partner and genuine colleague in our efforts to find solutions for the world's refugees. Above all, she has helped to make the tragedy of refugees real to everyone who will listen. Angelina's interest in helping refugees, her personal generosity, and her truly compassionate spirit are an inspiration to us all," he wrote.

Jolie donated all of the profits from the book's sale to UNHCR. She also dedicated the book to

On a 2003 visit to the Lugufu camp in Tanzania, Jolie plays games with some of the camp's older children. During her visit, Jolie also helped to build huts at the refugee camp.

UNHCR field workers and to the refugees themselves. In part, the dedication reads, "To the men, women, and children who are now or have once been refugees: to those who have survived against remarkable odds and to those who did not, those who died fighting for their freedom."

Jolie and Pitt have even teamed up together to produce their first television project. Pitched to HBO, the show is a drama that will go behind the scenes of an international aid organization, following field workers who put their lives in danger to help others. According to the *Hollywood Reporter*, the project has been of interest to Jolie since she starred in 2003's *Beyond Borders*, a movie about aid workers in war-torn Africa.

Jolie's Tireless Efforts Continue

Jolie works diligently to aid people worldwide. Her efforts as a Goodwill Ambassador will continue to bring her face to face with refugees. She will also continue to visit Capitol Hill to try to help pass legislation and seek funding for the protection and safety of children, and for relief aid for countries struggling to provide food and medicine for their people. She

may be an award-winning actress, but at the end of the day, Angelina Jolie's desire is to have made a powerful impact on the world. She has said in numerous interviews that what she would like to be remembered for is her work as a Goodwill Ambassador, to know that she has done some good in the world. And by all accounts, she has.

GLOSSARY

AIDS (acquired immunodeficiency syndrome) A disease caused by the human immunodeficiency virus (HIV), which researchers believe originated in sub-Saharan Africa during the twentieth century.

asylum A form of protection that allows refugees to remain in another country.

bipartisan Represented or supported by two parties.

Congressional bill A legislative proposal sent before Congress, where it is voted on.

de-miners People or organizations that work to clear land mines.

desertification The change of land into a desert either from natural causes or human activity.

genocide The deliberate and systematic destruction of an ethnic, religious, or national group.

humanitarian A person promoting human welfare and social reform.

indigenous Originating in and typical of a country or region.

lobbyist A person who promotes a particular interest to government officials of the Senate and Congress. A lobbyist can also work to change public opinion through advertising campaigns or by influencing leaders to take action.

malaria A disease transmitted via the bite of an infected mosquito. Symptoms usually appear between ten and fifteen days after the bite and include fever, headache, and vomiting. If not treated, malaria can quickly become life-threatening.

mandated Authoritatively ordered or demanded.

Nobel Peace Prize Named for Swedish inventor Alfred Nobel, the prize is awarded to a person or organization that works to promote peace within and among nations.

peacekeeping As defined by the United Nations, a way to help countries torn by conflict create conditions for sustainable peace. Peacekeepers monitor and observe peace processes in post-conflict areas and assist ex-combatants in implementing peace agreements.

refugee A person who flees to a foreign country to escape danger or persecution.

secretary of state The head of the U.S. Department of State, which is concerned with foreign affairs. The secretary is a member of the president's cabinet. He or she is the highest-ranking cabinet secretary both in line of succession and order of precedence.

sociopath A person suffering from behavior that is aggressively antisocial.

sub-Saharan Africa The area of the African continent that lies south of the Sahara Desert.

third world Underdeveloped nations, especially those located in Latin America, Africa, and Asia. Third world nations share common characteristics, such as poverty, high birthrates, and economic dependence on more advanced nations, such as the United States and countries in Europe.

United Nations (UN) A global organization with headquarters in New York City that works to maintain international peace and security.

United Nations secretary-general The head of the Secretariat, one of the principal arms of the UN. The secretary-general acts as the de facto spokesperson and leader of the UN.

wildlife sanctuary An area protected from humans where animals may live without the threat of being hunted.

FOR MORE INFORMATION

Amnesty International Canada
312 Laurier Avenue East
Ottawa, ON K1N 1H9
Canada
(800) AMNESTY (266-3789) or (613) 744-7667
Web site: http://www.amnesty.ca
The mission of Amnesty International Canada is
 based on human rights issues both in Canada
 and around the world.

The Earth Institute at Columbia University
405 Low Library, MC 4335
535 West 116th Street
New York, NY 10027
(845) 365-8565
Web site: http://www.earth.columbia.edu
The Earth Institute's goal is to help achieve sustainable
 development primarily by expanding the world's
 understanding of Earth as one integrated system.

The HALO Trust
P.O. Box 7905

Thornhill, DG3 5WA
United Kingdom
Web site: http://www.halotrust.org
HALO Trust is a British organization that specializes
in the removal of land mines.

Mine Action Information Center
James Madison University
MSC 4018
51B Burgess Road
Harrisonburg, VA 22807
(540) 568-2756
Web site: http://maic.jmu.edu
The Mine Action Information Center is a public policy
center that manages information and conducts
training relevant to humanitarian mine clearance,
victim assistance, mine risk reduction, and other
landmine-related issues.

United Nations Headquarters (UN)
First Avenue at 46th Street
New York, NY 10017
Web site: http://www.un.org/english

The UN is a global association of governments that facilitates cooperation in international law, security, economic development, and social equity.

United Nations High Commissioner for Refugees (UNHCR)
Case Postale 2500
CH-1211 Geneva 2 Dépôt
Switzerland
Web site: http://www.unhcr.org
This UN agency is mandated to lead and coordinate international action to protect refugees and resolve refugee problems worldwide.

Web Sites

Due to the changing nature of Internet links, Rosen Publishing has developed an online list of Web sites related to the subject of this book. This site is updated regularly. Please use this link to access the list:

http://www.rosenlinks.com/cea/anjo

FOR FURTHER READING

Bixler, Mark. *The Lost Boys of Sudan: An American Story of the Refugee Experience*. Athens, GA: The University of Georgia Press, 2005.

Dau, John Bul, and Michael S. Sweeney. *God Grew Tired of Us: A Memoir*. Washington, DC: National Geographic, 2007.

Jolie, Angelina. *Notes from My Travels: Visits with Refugees in Africa, Cambodia, Pakistan, and Ecuador*. New York, NY: Pocket Books, 2003.

Mercer, Rhona. *Angelina Jolie: The Biography*. London, England: John Blake Publishing, 2007.

Naido, Beverley. *Making It Home: Real-Life Stories from Children Forced to Flee*. New York, NY: Puffin Books, 2005.

Pearl, Mariane. *A Mighty Heart: The Inside Story of the Al Qaeda Kidnapping of Danny Pearl*. New York, NY: Scribner, 2003.

Springer, Jane. *Genocide* (Groundwork Guides). Toronto, ON: Groundwood Books, 2007.

BIBLIOGRAPHY

Aarsaether, Paal. "Swedish Teenagers Raise US$800,000 to Help Congolese Refugee Students." UNHCR News Stories. September 21, 2006. Retrieved August 22, 2007 (http://www.unhcr.org/cgi-bin/texis/vtx/news/opendoc.htm?tbl=NEWS&id=4512b0e34).

Aarsaether, Paal. "Thousands of Swedish Teenagers Collect Money for Refugee Schools in Rwanda." UNHCR News Stories. May 10, 2006. Retrieved August 22, 2007 (http://www.unhcr.org/news/NEWS/446211612.html).

ABC News. "Angelina Jolie Targets World Hunger." *Good Morning America*. September 13, 2005. Retrieved August 22, 2007 (http://abcnews.go.com/GMA/story?id=1120954).

Access Hollywood. "Angelina Jolie Commits to World's Children." May 4, 2007. Retrieved August 23, 2007 (http://www.msnbc.msn.com/id/18425828).

Anderson Cooper 360°. "Angelina Jolie: Her Mission and Motherhood." Transcript. Aired June 20, 2006. Retrieved August 14, 2007 (http://www.

transcripts.cnn.com/TRANSCRIPTS/0606/20/acd.01.html).

"Angelina Jolie Adopts a Daughter." *People*. July 6, 2005. Retrieved October 1, 2007 (http://www.people.com/people/article/0,26334,1079776,00.html).

"Angelina Jolie Calls for Action." *People*. April 19, 2006. Retrieved September 11, 2007 (http://www.people.com/people/article/0,,1185087,00.html).

BBC News. "Country Profile: Sierre Leone." Retrieved September 13, 2007 (http://news.bbc.co.uk/2/hi/africa/country_profiles/1061561.stm).

BBC News. "Jolie and Pitt Fund Sudan Clinic." Retrieved October 2007 (http://news.bbc.co.uk/2/hi/entertainment/6486093.stm).

BBC News. "Jolie Given Cambodian Citizenship." August 12, 2005. Retrieved September 9, 2007 (http://news.bbc.co.uk/2/hi/entertainment/4144518.stm).

CBS News. "Pitt, Jolie Donate to Pearl Foundation." Showbuzz.com. October 10, 2006. Retrieved September 11, 2007 (http://www.showbuzz.cbsnews.com/stories/2006/10/10/people_crusades/main2077328.shtml).

CNN.com. "World Refugee Day." 2007. Retrieved September 9, 2007 (http://edition.cnn.com/CNN/Programs/refugee.day).

Dickey, Christopher. "'I Was Transformed.'" *Newsweek*. March 11, 2007. Retrieved September 10, 2007 (http://www.msnbc.msn.com/id/17540069/site/newsweek).

Doctors Without Borders. "What Is Doctors Without Borders?" Retrieved October 2007 (http://www.doctorswithoutborders.org/aboutus).

Green, Mary. "Angelina: I'm the 'Luckiest.'" *People*. November 18, 2005. Retrieved October 1, 2007 (http://www.people.com/people/article/0,,1132438,00.html).

Green, Mary. "Angelina Jolie Joins Council on Foreign Relations." *People*. June 7, 2007. Retrieved August 9, 2007 (http://www.people.com/people/article/0,,20041839,00.html).

Green, Mary. "Brad & Angelina Start Charitable Group." *People*. September 20, 2006. Retrieved September 9, 2007 (http://www.people.com/people/article/0,26334,1537302,00.html).

Green, Mary, and Kat Johnson. "It's Official: Angelina Jolie Adopts New Son." *People*. March 15, 2007.

Retrieved October 1, 2007 (http://www.people.com/people/article/0,,20014961,00.html).

Haley, Kathleen. "Testimony of Hope." *Syracuse University Magazine*, Fall 2006, Vol. 23, No. 3.

Jolie, Angelina. "Justice for Darfur." *Washington Post.* February 28, 2007. Retrieved August 8, 2007 (http://www.washingtonpost.com/wp-dyn/content/article/2007/02/27/AR2007022701161.html).

Kirkland, Bruce. "The New Angelina Jolie." Canoe.ca. October 19, 2003. Retrieved September 9, 2007 (http://www.jam.canoe.ca/Movies/Artists/J/Jolie_Angelina/2003/10/19/759420.html).

Lange, Jenny. "An Interview with Angelina Jolie." *Landmines in Africa.* August 2002. Retrieved September 21, 2007 (http://maic.jmu.edu/journal/6.2/notes/jennylange/jennylange.htm).

Mayell, Hillary. "Angelina Jolie on Her UN Refugee Role." *National Geographic News.* June 18, 2003. Retrieved August 23, 2007 (http://news.nationalgeographic.com/news/2003/06/0618_030618_angelinajolie.html).

Mayell, Hillary. "Refugee Children, Victims of War and Want." *National Geographic News.* June 19, 2003. Retrieved September 13, 2007 (http://

news.nationalgeographic.com/news/2003/06/
0619_030618_refugeechildren.html).

Miller, Prairie. "Angelina Jolie on Filling Lara Croft's Shoes and D-Size Cups." NY Rock. June 2001. Retrieved October 2007 (http://www.nyrock.com/ interviews/2001/jolie_int.asp).

MTV. "The Diary of Angelina Jolie and Dr. Jeffrey Sachs in Africa." Think MTV. 2006. Retrieved September 14, 2007 (http://www.mtv.com/ thinkmtv/global/diary/angelina_jolie).

Norman, Pete. "Angelina 'Transformed' by Work with Refugees." *People*. March 12, 2007. Retrieved September 9, 2007 (http://www. people.com/people/article/0,,20014723,00.html).

Refugees International. "World Refugee Day: Angelina Jolie & Ken Bacon Speak on Capitol Hill." June 21, 2003. Retrieved October 2007 (http://www. refugeesinternational.org/content/article/detail/1522).

Silverman, Stephen M. "Angelina Jolie Calls for More Funding for Orphans." *People*. April 26, 2007. Retrieved September 11, 2007 (http://www.people. com/people/article/0,,20036908,00.html).

Silverman, Stephen M. "Angelina Takes Cameras to Kenya." *People*. August 16, 2005. Retrieved

August 23, 2007 (http://www.people.com/people/article/0,,1094286,00.html).

Swibel, Matthew. "Bad Girl Interrupted." Forbes.com. July 3, 2006. Retrieved September 10, 2007 (http://www.forbes.com/forbes/2006/0703/118_print.html).

UNHCR. "Angelina Jolie and UNHCR Promote Education at Clinton Global Initiative." UNHCR Special Events. Retrieved September 9, 2007 (http://www.unhcr.org/events/46e7db842.html).

UNHCR. "Angelina Jolie, Business Leaders Help UNHCR Improve Life for World's Refugees." UNHCR Press Release. January 27, 2005. Retrieved September 27, 2007 (http://www.unhcr.org/news/NEWS/41f8dbee4.html).

UNHCR. "Angelina Jolie Hears Stories of Suffering, Courage from Iraqi Refugees." UNHCR News. August 29, 2007. Retrieved September 11, 2007 (http://www.unhcr.org/news/NEWS/46d544c16.html).

UNHCR. "Angelina Jolie Named UNHCR Goodwill Ambassador for Refugees." UNHCR Press Release. August 23, 2001. Retrieved October 1, 2007 (http://www.unhcr.org/news/NEWS/3b85044b10.html).

UNHCR. "Goodwill Ambassador Angelina Jolie Accepts Global Humanitarian Award." UNHCR News Stories. October 13, 2005. Retrieved October 2007 (http://www.unhcr.org/news/NEWS/434e17b84.html).

UNHCR. "Jolie Discusses Unaccompanied Children with US Senior Officials." UNHCR News Stories. May 27, 2004. Retrieved October 1, 2007 (http://www.unhcr.org/news/NEWS/40b5f58f4.html).

UNHCR. "Jolie Thanks Tanzania for Longstanding Support to Refugees." UNHCR News Stories. April 2, 2003. Retrieved October 1, 2007 (http://www.unhcr.org/news/NEWS/3e8b1c315.html).

UNHCR. "UNHCR Joins Hands with Top Business Leaders to Help Refugees." UNHCR News Stories. January 28, 2005. Retrieved October 1, 2007 (http://www.unhcr.org/news/NEWS/41fa5cdf4.html).

UNHCR. "Urgent Funds Needed for Darfur Refugees, Stresses Jolie." UNHCR News Stories. June 7, 2004. Retrieved October 1, 2007 (http://www.unhcr.org/news/NEWS/40c4694f4.html).

UN News Centre. "Jolie-Pitt Foundation Donates $1 Million to UN and Other Groups Working in

Darfur." May 11, 2007. Retrieved September 11, 2007 (http://www.un.org/apps/news/story.asp? NewsID=22520&Cr=Darfur&Cr1=).

U.S. Committee for Refugees and Immigrants. "About the Center." Retrieved October 2007 (http://www.refugees.org/article.aspx?id=1408& subm=75&area=Participate&ssm=85).

Van Meter, Jonathan. "Body Beautiful." Style.com: *Vogue* Feature Story. 2002. Retrieved September 9, 2007 (http://www.style.com/vogue/feature/ 032602/page2.html).

Van Meter, Jonathan. "Learning to Fly." Style.com: *Vogue* Feature Story. 2004. Retrieved September 9, 2007 (http://www.style.com/vogue/ feature/022304/page2.html).

INDEX

About the Author

Laura La Bella is a writer who lives and works in Rochester, New York. La Bella and her husband, a social studies teacher, are active in organizations that support breast cancer research, prevent animal cruelty, and promote the arts.

Photo Credits

Cover, p. 1 © J. Redden/UNHCR/Getty Images, cover (inset) © Chris Jackson/Getty Images; pp. 5, 17, 22, 35, 45, 48 © AP Images; p. 10 Jerry Ohlinger's; p. 12 © Doug Niven/AFP/Getty Images; p. 19 © Seyllou Diallo/AFP/Getty Images; p. 26 © Jean Ayissi/AFP/Getty Images; pp. 29, 90–91 © Natalie Behring-Chisholm/Getty Images; p. 31 © Morris Bernard/AFP/Getty Images; p. 33 © Antony Njuguna/Reuters/Landov; p. 39 © Alex Wong/Getty Images; p. 42 © Evan Agostini/Getty Images; p. 52 © Chor Sokunthea/Reuters/Landov; pp. 54–55 © UNHCR/Getty Images; p. 57 © Moses Muiruri/Reuters/Landov; p. 61 © Fabrice Coffrini/AFP/Getty Images; p. 66 © Scott J. Ferrell/Congressional Quarterly/Getty Images; p. 68 © Nicholas Kamm/AFP/Getty Images; p. 70 © Win McNamee/Getty Images; p. 75 © Karen Bleier/AFP/Getty Images; p. 77 © AFP/Getty Images; p. 80 © Ron Haviv/VII/AP Images; p. 83 © Kevin Winter/Getty Images; p. 87 © Matt Cardy/Getty Images.

Designer: Tahara Anderson; Photo Researcher: Amy Feinberg